The Truth About ... The Bible

Should I Believe Everything The Bible Says?

There is an old saying that "What you don't know can't hurt you." Maybe you have heard it like this: "Ignorance is bliss." Well, ignorance is not bliss, especially when it comes to the Bible. I know because I have been there.

There was a time in my life when I just accepted as absolute truth whatever I heard about the Bible or happened to read in it. I never gave much thought to what it was saying and why. And so, I ended up confused and frustrated.

Countless lives have been hurt because people have just accepted as absolute truth what they have heard about or read in the Bible. Most church people are taught to believe that everything in the Bible, from Genesis to Revelation, is the unmitigated truth. They are under the impression that you are supposed to simply take the Bible at face value without much, if any, thought. And if they don't, it's almost as if they are not sincere in their beliefs. What I — and so many others like me — failed to see was that you can believe in the Bible and believe the wrong thing. You can be sincere, and still be sincerely wrong.

The Book of Job gives a good example of this in the account of Job losing

The Truth About ...
The Bible

Should I Believe Everything the Bible Says?

**By
Frederick K.C. Price, D.D.**

**Faith One Publishing
Los Angeles, California**

Unless otherwise indicated, all Scripture quotations are taken from *The New King James Version*. Copyright © 1979, 1980, 1982, Thomas Nelson, Inc., Publishers. Used by permission.

The Truth About . . . The Bible:
Should I Believe Everything the Bible Says?
ISBN 1-883798-38-8

Copyright © 1999 by
Frederick K.C. Price, D.D.
P.O. Box 90000
Los Angeles, CA 90009

Published by Faith One Publishing
7901 South Vermont Avenue
Los Angeles, California 90044

Printed in the United States of America. All rights reserved under International Copyright Law. Contents and/or cover may not be reproduced in whole or in part, in any form or by any means, without the express written consent of the Publisher.

everything he owned. Even Job's children were killed. He was left with nothing. Yet, Job still loved the Lord. Job's response to all of the calamities that had come upon him is recorded in Job 1:20-21:

> **Then Job arose, tore his robe, and shaved his head; and he fell to the ground and worshipped.**
>
> **And he said: "Naked I came from my mother's womb, and naked shall I return there.** *The Lord gave, and the Lord has taken away; blessed be the name of the Lord."*

Chances are, if you have ever been to a funeral, you are at least somewhat familiar with this Scripture. Too often, particularly in a eulogy, a minister will quote, **"The**

LORD gave, and the LORD has taken away; blessed be the name of the LORD." The impression given when the officiating minister quotes this verse is that God did it; God took your loved one. Most people have simply accepted this statement as fact, but it bears closer examination.

Job's Mistake

Let's take a look at the context from which this popular quote was taken. In Job 1:6-12, the Bible records what happened before Job lost everything:

> Now there was a day when the sons of God came to present themselves before the LORD, and Satan also came among them.

And the Lord said to Satan, "From where do you come?" So Satan answered the Lord and said, "From going to and fro on the earth, and from walking back and forth on it."

Then the Lord said to Satan, "Have you considered My servant Job, that there is none like him on the earth, a blameless and upright man, one who fears God and shuns evil?"

So Satan answered the Lord and said, "Does Job fear God for nothing?

"Have You not made a hedge around him, around his household, and around all that he has on every side? You have blessed the work of his hand, and his possessions have increased in the land.

"But now, stretch out Your hand and touch all that he has, and he will surely curse You to Your face!"

And the LORD said to Satan, "Behold, all that he has is in your power; only do not lay a hand on his person." So Satan went out from the presence of the LORD.

It was shortly after this that everything Job had was stolen from him. But contrary to what Job thought, this Scripture says that God was not the one who took everything from Job — Satan was.

So what Job said about the calamities that had come upon him was wrong. What he said was spoken out of ignorance, and his assessment of the situation gives the wrong impression of God. If you do not see that Job was mistaken, you will not be able to see God as the loving Father that He so very much wants to be to you. So you see, ignorance is not bliss!

Yet, this verse is misused all the time. It is unfortunate, but there are multitudes of verses like this throughout the Bible that are often either misused or misquoted. So, how do you know what to believe about what you read in the Bible?

Given by Inspiration of God

In 2 Timothy 3:16, the Apostle Paul gives His spiritual son, Timothy, important insight into understanding the nature of the

Bible that can help us know what to believe. Paul writes:

> **All Scripture is given by inspiration of God, and is profitable for doctrine, for reproof, for correction, for instruction in righteousness....**

Look closely at what this verse does not say. I call this my "flip-flop" method of studying the Bible; oftentimes, it is easier to see what a passage of Scripture is saying by first realizing what it does not say. Paul does not say that all Scripture *is inspired*. By not saying that all Scripture — all of the Bible — is inspired, Paul is telling Timothy that the Lord God did not ordain everything in the Bible.

Saying that something is *given by inspiration* does not mean that what is given was necessarily inspired in and of itself. What it means is that the Father God obviously wanted you and I to know about it, so He inspired that it be written.

Inspiration comes from a Greek word meaning, "to breathe into." This is not how this word is used today, but the medical profession still uses its antonym, *expiration*, in its original context. *Expiration* means, "for the breath or air to go out." When a person dies, the medical record states that he or she *expired* at 7:15 a.m. By using the term *expired*, medical professionals are saying that the breath of life, or the life force, has gone out of the body. Conversely, by using the word *inspiration*, Paul is saying God breathed His Word, which is life, into the men who are generally said to have written the Bible. In other words, the Bible was not conceived by man.

The men of God who penned the Scriptures acted much like a court stenotypist does today in recording the official record of a legal case. God breathed His Word into men, who recorded what God had deposited in them. The official record of what God breathed into these men is contained in what we know as the Bible.

As you read the Bible, you will see that it is actually a record of God's relationship with mankind. Just as the court stenotypist is not responsible for what happens in the legal case, God did not ordain those things that He inspired to be recorded in the Bible. He simply dictated the account of His relationship with His people, Israel, —

including the good, the bad and even the ugly — so that it could be put on record. This is why Paul says that **All Scripture *is given by inspiration* of God**, and this is too important a revelation to overlook because it lets you know that not everything in the Bible can be taken and counted on as absolute truth.

Statements of Truth

I like to say what Paul is saying in 2 Timothy 3:16 like this: *"Everything in the Bible is truly stated, but not everything in the Bible is a statement of truth."* This is not double-talk. Let me give you a simple example that should clearly illustrate the difference between what is truly stated and what is a statement of truth.

Say you are the secretary and I am the president of the board of directors of the XYZ Corporation. During the annual stockholder's meeting, I call the meeting to order. I have you read the minutes of the last meeting. Next, we enter into the actual business, according to the agenda. In the course of the meeting, I make the statement, "All dogs have three heads and two tails." As the secretary, you record this statement in the minutes of the meeting.

A year passes, and you are still serving as the corporate secretary. Again, I open the stockholder's meeting with the reading of the minutes from the previous year. You rise and read the account of the prior meeting, and you quote me, President Frederick K.C. Price, as having said, "All dogs have three heads and two tails." Is this true?

Yes, it is true that I made the statement that, "All dogs have three heads and two tails," but what I said is not a statement of truth. Can you see the difference? The record of my having said, "All dogs have three heads and two tails" is indeed truly stated; it is truly recorded in the minutes. I did actually say this. But just because I said it does not make it true. In fact, I don't know of any dogs that have three heads and two tails. Certainly, it is clear that *all* dogs do not have three heads and two tails. So, this part of the minutes from the stockholder's meeting is not a statement of truth — it is only truly stated.

Just because you read something in the Bible does not automatically make what you have read a statement of truth and, therefore, something you should say or do.

You have to know who said it and why. If you don't know, you could be looking for a dog with three heads and two tails that does not exist.

How Can I Know What to Believe?

All the way through the Bible you can see how, as man was able to comprehend more of the things of God, God revealed more facets of His plan for mankind. Through His prophets and leaders, the Lord God gave His people revelation that was collected and collated into the Old and New Testaments.

Sometimes this revelation had only immediate value and direction to those who initially received it. Other times, the **revelation was for the future, like the** prophesies given of the coming of Jesus Christ. There were also times when the revelation was universal, meaning that it was applicable at that time, now, and in the future.

Most people do not give thought to the fact that different parts of the Bible were written to different groups of people at different times. They do not realize that while the Old Testament was initially written for the children of Israel, parts of it applied to the world at large. Most of the New Testament, on the other hand, was written specifically to those who are Christian. However, parts of it do apply to those who have yet to receive Jesus Christ as their personal Savior and Lord, while other parts pertain to the Jewish people. So, part of accurately discerning what you can and should believe about a Scripture requires us to ask, "To whom is this Scripture directed?"

As I mentioned, the majority of the Old Testament was written to and about the children of Israel, and it remains a viable part of the Bible. But, under the Old Covenant, God established the use of animal sacrifices to get rid of sin. Back then, every type of sin against God had a corresponding sacrifice that would bring man back into right status with Him. This was necessary because, as a law established by God in the Old Testament (Leviticus 17:11) states, there is no remission of sin without the shedding of blood. In other words, there is a price to be paid for sin, and that price is blood.

Now, if you have only read the Old Testament, you might not know that this system of sacrifice is no longer in effect. You and I cannot go kill a dog or a cat and take it before the Lord God and say, "I give you this dog, Lord, as an offering for the sin I committed last week." No. This will no longer work. God is not going to accept this as a way to be reconciled to Him.

How do you know what I am saying is true? Because the New Testament says that Jesus Christ is the Lamb of God who took away the sin of the world. You and I are under the age of the New Testament, which dictates that salvation is through no one other than Jesus Christ. But if all you know is the Old Testament, you might think that the old system of animal sacrifice will still work for you.

This brings me to my next point. Part of learning what you can and should believe about what you read in the Bible takes understanding that the Old Testament is a foundation for the New Testament. Since God used Israel to bring into manifestation His plan and purpose for mankind, the Old Testament, which is the history of the Lord's relationship with the children of Israel, is coupled with the New Testament as one complete book. Obviously, since we have the New Testament, it supersedes the Old. But we still need to be able to draw from the Old Covenant so that we can better understand the New Testament.

As you read about the initiation of this sacrifice system, you can see a revelation of the heart of God — that He desires that no man would perish or spend eternity apart from Him, but be reconciled to Him. This is reaffirmed in the New Testament; 2 Peter

3:9 says that God is not willing that any should perish but that all should come to repentance.

In order to know what you can and should believe in the Bible, you also need to recognize that there are spiritual laws that the Lord established at the foundation of the world that are still in effect today, and that references to these laws are made throughout the Scripture. Deuteronomy 28 is one such example. There are blessings and the curses revealed in the Old Covenant that are the result of these laws.

One main law is the law of sowing and reaping. This law is found both in the Old Testament in Genesis 8:22 and in the New Testament in Galatians 6:7. Basically, it assures that whatever a man sows, he will also reap. Even to this day, you can see how those who are diligent to obey the voice of the Lord God prosper and enjoy peace. Obedience produces blessings, while disobedience eventually leads to destruction.

How do you know what in the Bible is a revelation of these laws? A particular Scripture either refers to or is a spiritual or natural law because it has universal application. It will prove just as true and relevant today as it did when it was first recorded in the Word of God, just like the law of sowing and reaping. You can trust that these laws will work for you when you cooperate with them, and that they will work against you when you violate them.

You cannot simply pull any Scripture out of the Bible and expect it to be the absolute truth and therefore work for you without first weighing it in terms of the context in which it is given. A good example illustrating this point lies in understanding that the Old Testament was originally written in Hebrew, while the New Testament was written primarily in Greek. And each book of the Bible was initially written in the form of a continuous narrative printed on long scrolls of papyrus. All the letters were capitalized. No grammatical punctuation or chapter and verse designations were marked. There were no lowercase lettering or commas or periods.

When the various scholars translated the Bible, they wanted to put the Bible into a format that everyone could easily read. So, they added punctuation and transcribed the lettering into both uppercase and lowercase.

They also divided the biblical narrative into chapters and verses.

Unlike those who originally penned the Word of God, these translators may or may not have been working under the inspiration of God. After all, they primarily were academic scholars, many of whom had their own conceptions of what the Bible says or should say. Their religious viewpoints and ethnic backgrounds could not help but have influenced their work.

This is why you must keep in mind as you read and study the Bible that it was the words, not the punctuation marks, chapter breaks, or the verse and lowercase and uppercase designations that were given by the inspiration of God. So you may even have to disregard these because **even the smallest change** from what was originally intended can alter the entire meaning of a Scripture.

There are even discrepancies in the translation of some words from the original text. This is where good study aids, as well as knowing the character of God, will help you know the truth about what you are reading.

In the ancient Hebrew language from which the Old Testament largely came, there is both the permissive and the causative point of view expressed with verbs. Many scholars translated the majority of the Old Testament from the causative point of view. Consequently, the English translation often reads as if God is the cause of the horrible things that happened to His people, rather than simply having permitted the spiritual and natural laws He had established to function. Throughout the English version of the Old Testament, the Lord is supposedly telling His people that He will cause certain calamities to strike them. But this really would not have been necessary; Israel's violation of the spiritual and natural laws that He had already put into effect would do this without His intervention.

In other words, what hurt the disobedient children of Israel was a natural result of their violation of spiritual and natural laws. So, the Lord God simply *permitted* these consequences to take place; He did not actually *cause* them. However, you would not necessarily know this unless you remain aware that spiritual and natural laws do exist and govern our lives.

Deuteronomy 28 illustrates this point. In English, this Scripture passage reads as though God is saying that He will cause curses to come upon the children of Israel if they fail to obey His Word. This cannot be. God cannot send a curse because He does not have any curses in Him. He has only blessings; this is His nature, as recorded throughout the rest of the Bible.

The New Testament Book of James specifically says, **That every good and perfect gift comes down from the Father of Lights** (James 1:17). So, anything that is not perfect could not come from God because James 3:11 goes on to say that both sweet and bitter water cannot flow from the same source. God merely allows a curse to come on you if you do not obey His Word. But this is certainly not His will for you.

A little deductive reasoning will prove this to you. If God wanted you cursed, then

He would never have told you how to be blessed at the beginning of Deuteronomy 28. That would have messed up His plan. Still, there are many Scriptures, particularly in the Old Testament, that read as though God killed someone or did some horrible thing. But, for the most part, the Lord God only allowed or permitted what happened, and it was the result of the way His people were acting.

There is, however, one exception. This exception has to do with the few times that the Lord moved in judgment, as with the flood. You can tell which Scriptures these are because He simply wiped out everyone because of the sin they were continually perpetrating without heeding His plea for them to turn from their wicked ways.

Dividing the Word of Truth

Properly discerning what in the Bible is truly stated and what is a statement of truth is what determines whether you walk in prosperity or poverty, divine health or sickness and disease, peace and joy or confusion and frustration, or in victory or defeat. The heavenly Father wants the best for you. This is why He commands in 2 Timothy 2:15:

Be diligent to present yourself approved to God, a worker who does not need to be ashamed, rightly dividing the word of truth.

I believe the traditional King James translation of 2 Timothy 2:15 is more plain. It says:

Study to shew thyself approved unto God, a workman that needeth not to be ashamed, rightly dividing the word of truth.

The words *rightly dividing* come from the Greek word *orthotomeo,* which literally means "to make a straight cut, as in dissecting or expounding correctly." The fact that this Scripture specifically says *rightly dividing the word of truth* tells you that there must be a possibility of wrongly dividing the Scriptures.

Being able to rightly divide the Bible is important because, believe it or not, you have an adversary. He is the one behind the challenges you face in this life. His modus operandi is to kill, steal, and destroy. He is not your friend. He preys on your ignorance.

Ignorance of who he is and how he operates can leave you wide open to his attacks.

Now, you may say, "Well, I don't believe in the devil." This only makes it easier for him to steal from you and to ultimately kill and destroy you. Whether you believe he exists or not does not change the fact that he is real any more than not believing in gravity will stop its pull on you.

You need to recognize that there is no tactic that is too low for him to try in order to inflict some harm or damage on you. He will even try to use the Bible itself to cause you to doubt the veracity of God's Word. If you do not have proper understanding of a Bible verse, he will surely twist it to use it against you. He will have you believing the heavenly Father is responsible for the harm that he himself is actually imposing upon you. And if you think all the pain you are going through is of God, then you will not take the necessary steps to put an end to it. At best, you will just go right on hoping and praying that it will go away, while the devil steals, kills, and destroys you.

Just like Job, ignorance of God and the Bible can lead you to draw the wrong conclusions about the Lord. While the first chapter of the Book of Job reveals who the real culprit was behind all the calamities that struck Job, as the Scripture unfolds you can see the part Job played in his own demise. Job is quoted as saying in Job 3:25:

"For the thing I greatly feared has come upon me, and what I dreaded has happened to me."

Job feared losing his children and possessions. Fear is the absence of faith; faith is believing in and acting on God's Word. Whenever you don't trust God and do what His Word says, you are open to the devices of Satan. And you have no defense against him.

Think about it: How can you, in your own natural ability, withstand the supernatural power of Satan? You can't, unless you tap into the power of God through believing and acting on what His Word says. In other words, it is through faith that you are able to overcome the attacks of Satan. This is why the Lord said that all Job had was already in Satan's power. The Lord God did not say that He was giving this power to Satan, but merely pointed out that Satan already had it.

Because of Job's fear, Satan had an open door to wreak havoc in Job's life.

But because Job did not know that Satan was behind all the great calamities that he was facing, and because he did not understand how he had inadvertently given Satan access to steal from him, Job mistakenly assumed that God was behind all that had happened. Ignorance can likewise lead you to think that the Father God is punishing you when, in actuality, the enemy has come in to steal, kill, and destroy.

Believing what Job says — that **"The Lord gave, and the Lord has taken away…"** — just because you see it written in the Bible stabs right at the heart of God and destroys your ability to trust God. If you are left thinking that the Lord "gives and then takes away," how can you ever believe that He wants the best for you?

So, you have to know that Satan is the thief, not God. Jesus said in John 10:10:

> **"The thief does not come except to steal, and to kill, and to destroy. I have come that they may have life, and that they may have it more abundantly."**

This Scripture clearly says that Satan is the one who kills, not God. But if you don't know this Scripture, Satan can make you afraid of, or angry with God and cause you to be in doubt, guilt, and condemnation. All of these emotions cut you off from God, leaving you completely susceptible to Satan's whims.

Jesus, the Second Person of the Godhead, says that He (God) gives life, and gives it more abundantly — he doesn't take it. But you have to know that God will allow or permit things to be taken from you — *if* you allow or permit it. He has to, because He has given you the very precious gift of a free will. He has given you the ability to determine your life. So if God were to just step into your life and take over when Satan attacks, then He would be in violation of that precious gift — the ability to control your own life.

But you have not been left helpless. By accepting Jesus Christ as the Lord of your life, you have all the authority and power you need to carry out your free will. Look at what Jesus says to His disciples in Luke 10:19:

"Behold, I give you the authority to trample on serpents and scorpions, and over all the power of the enemy, and nothing shall by any means hurt you."

So, if you believe in Jesus and follow His ways for your life, you have been given the authority and the responsibility to do something about Satan. If you do not do anything when Satan sets out to rob, kill, or destroy, then he will have his way with you and there is nothing God can do about it because the choice, authority, and power over your life have been given to you.

The Proof Is in the Results

Going back to 2 Timothy 3:16, Paul gives his spiritual son, Timothy, an important revelation about the Scripture that I believe is the acid test for knowing if what you believe about a particular Scripture verse is in fact accurate and true. The Apostle Paul, who wrote two-thirds of the New Testament, says that **All Scripture is given by inspiration of God and *is* profitable**....

Paul says that the Scripture is profitable. When you *profit,* you gain something. If a thing profits you, then you should be the better for it. In the financial world, you hear of profit-and-loss statements. When you have a loss, it is bad news; when you have a profit, it is good news. Well, the Gospel of Jesus Christ is good news; the word *gospel* literally means the good news. In this Scripture Paul is assuring Timothy of just that the Word of God is meant to better your life, not leave you struggling.

This still holds true today. Paul did not tell Timothy that the Scripture was only profitable to him or during his lifetime. No. Paul said that the Scripture is profitable. The Scripture is and will always be profitable. This means that you and I can and should benefit from it as well.

This tells me that if you are not profiting from what you believe a particular Scripture passage says, then you need to check up on what you have been believing. You will have to take time to read and study the Word of God for yourself. You will have to train yourself to read exactly what God's Word literally says, and not what tradition or religious theology has told you it says. Then you will have to put what you have learned into practice. As you do, you will gain wisdom and practical insight into the things of God that will profit you.

Finding out for yourself what God says is so important that the Lord God instructed Joshua, as he was about to take over the leadership of the nation of Israel and lead the nation into the Promised Land,

> **"This Book of the Law shall not depart from your mouth, but you shall meditate in it day and night, that you may observe to do according to all that is written in it. For then you will make your way prosperous, and then you will have good success."**

The Lord God told Joshua to not ever let the Word of God depart from his mouth — in other words, he was only to speak those things which are in line with God's Word. Joshua was not to let the Word of God depart in the sense of letting go of God's Word. He was to hold onto God's Word by speaking it.

The Lord God also instructed Joshua to meditate in the Word of God day and night. Joshua knew that this meant that God's Word was to be his lifestyle. And then the Lord told him to observe to do. Now, this is real wisdom. God is saying that you should not do anything until you first observe it in order to see what will result from what you have to do.

By employing these three very basic instructions, the Bible says you will not only have success, but that you will have *good* success. And, did you notice that it says that *you* make your way prosperous? God doesn't do it for you. You make your own way prosperous by always keeping God's Word before you as your guide.

The Lord God did not tell Joshua to go find out from His people what the Word of God has to say. He did not even tell Joshua to go find a prophet or a minister to tell him "What thus saith the Lord." No. Joshua was instructed to find out for himself. The same is true for you. You have to check the Scriptures for yourself.

Here's your example. Acts 17:11 says:

These were [those in Berea] **more fair-minded than those in Thessalonica, in that they received**

the word with all readiness, and searched the Scriptures daily to find out whether these things [what Paul and Silas taught them] **were so.**

The Lord calls the people in Berea more fair-minded because they took the time to not only hear the Word of God proclaimed, but they went and searched and studied the Scriptures to see for themselves if what they had heard was true.

Unfortunately, few people — even Christians — follow this example. Some so-called Christians will not even take the time to go hear what "Thus saith the Lord." Others will just accept whatever they hear coming from the pulpit as the Gospel truth. Neither of these approaches to the Bible will profit you. Ministers of the Gospel can make mistakes, just like you. I know because I made mistakes at times. This is why I insist that members of my congregation bring their Bibles to church services and that they study for themselves what I am saying. This is being fair-minded.

And finally, recognize that you cannot expect to know everything about the Word of God all at once. The revelation of God is progressive. His revelation to mankind was given over a long period of years, even though you now have it all chronicled in the Bible.

It is going to take time, time invested in studying and reading both the Bible and about the Bible, before you will come to know what you can and should believe. Then you have to actually apply what you have learned. As you see what you believe about the Bible working to your profit in your life, you will have the confirmation that you need.

Is the Bible Really God's Word?

As a minister of the Gospel, people often ask me "How do you know the Bible is really God's Word?" So I ask them "Well, how do you know the Bible is not the Word of God?" If you are honestly wondering if the Bible really is the Word of God, then I simply suggest you open it up and give what it says an opportunity to prove itself in your life.

Why not do as the psalmist says in Psalms 34:8, **Taste and see that the LORD is good**? What do you possibly have to lose?

You will never know if what the Bible says really works or if it truly is God's Word until you test it out for yourself by becoming a doer of the Word of God (James 1:22). There is so much the Bible promises New Covenant Believers that you simply have too much to lose by leaving this issue to mere speculation.

Saying, "Well, I don't believe the Bible" has no bearing on the reality of God's Word. After all, the lack of belief in gravity would not stop its effects. The force of gravity is at work and is directly affecting our lives regardless of what we may think or believe; we do not have to agree with gravity for it to affect us.

And the same is true with God's Word. Believing what God has said in His Word does not determine whether God's Word is true. God's Word is alive, true, and eternal regardless of what we believe, think, do, or have experienced; believing in the Word of God is not what determines its validity.

But, what is determined by what you believe in your heart and act upon is your ability to benefit from God's Word. It takes faith — acting on the Word of God — to bring God's Word to pass in your life. Otherwise, His Word will not benefit you. So, you will never know the Bible truly is the Word of God unless you follow its instructions and mix all of its ingredients into your life.

I have personally tested God's Word, not only see if it works, but to see if it will work for me. God's Word has proven reliable every time, without fail. Can you say this about yourself? Have you always been perfectly right in everything you have said or done in your life? Have you ever made a mistake? Are you sure that doubting the validity of God's Word is not another mistake? And can you really afford to make such a mistake?

You cannot afford to wait until you die to find out if God's Word is true. It will be too late then. Whether you believe there is a hell or not has no bearing on its existence. Hell is a real place. If you want to miss hell, you must do as God's Word says in Romans 10:9-10 and accept Jesus Christ as your personal Savior and Lord while you are still alive in your physical body. Otherwise, the decision of where you spend eternity will be made for you once you have physically died. And I guarantee that you will not like the decision. You owe it to yourself to examine the validity of God's Word now.

You will never know that the Bible is God's Word until you use it in your life every day. Once you begin to live by God's Word, the Bible will prove more real to you than what you see, hear, taste, smell, or even touch. It will change your life. There are no challenges that you will not be able to fix with the proper application of the Bible and the love and faith that goes along with walking by God's Word.

So pick up the Bible, read and study it for yourself. Don't just believe what you have heard that it says. Let God speak to you from the pages containing His Word. Then you will come to know what you should believe about everything the Bible says.

Prayer for Salvation

If you are not a Christian and would like to become one, I would like you to pray the following prayer:

Dear God:

Thank you for sending Your Son Jesus Christ to destroy the spiritual and the physical power of death over my life. I accept Jesus now as my personal Savior and Lord, and choose life by turning away from the sins of my past to a renewed life in Jesus.

You said that if I would confess with my mouth the Lord Jesus and believe in my heart that You raised Him from the dead, then I would be saved. I do that now. I believe Jesus died for my sin and that You raised Him from the dead for my benefit. So, I thank You for the gift of salvation and I thank You for accepting me now as Your child. In Jesus' name, Amen.

About the Author

Dr. Frederick K.C. Price is a world-renowned teacher of the biblical principles of faith, healing, prosperity and the Holy Spirit. During his more than 47 years in ministry, countless lives have been changed by his dynamic and insightful teachings that truly "tell it like it is."

His television program, *Ever Increasing Faith*, has been broadcast throughout the world for more than 20 years and airs in 15 of the 20 largest markets in America, reaching an audience of more than 15 million households each week. His radio program is heard on stations across the world, including the continent of Europe via shortwave radio.

Author of more than 50 popular books teaching practical application of biblical principles, Dr. Price is also the founder and pastor of one of America's largest church congregations, with a membership of more than 20,000. The church sanctuary, the

FaithDome, is among the most notable and largest in the nation, with seating capacity of more than 10,000.

In 1990, Dr. Price founded the Fellowship of Inner City Word of Faith Ministries (FICWFM) that comprises more than 300 ministries throughout the world.

Dr. Price holds an honorary Doctorate of Divinity degree from Oral Roberts University and an honorary diploma from Rhema Bible Training Center.

Dr. Frederick K.C. Price is a 1998 recipient of the Horatio Alger Award. Each year, this prestigious honor is bestowed upon ten "outstanding Americans who exemplify inspirational success, triumph over adversity, and an uncommon commitment to helping others...." He also received the 1998 Southern Christian Leadership Conference's Kelly Miller Smith Interfaith Award. This award is given to clergy who have made the most significant contribution through religious expression affecting the nation and the world.

Parts of this mini-book are taken from
a larger body of teaching entitled:

Beware! The Lies of Satan

Written by Dr. Frederick K.C. Price.

*Copies of these books
are available at local bookstores.*

To receive a catalog or be placed
on the EIF mailing list, please call:

(800) 927-3436

For more information, please write:

**Crenshaw Christian Center
P.O. Box 90000
Los Angeles, CA 90009**

or check your local TV listing:

**Ever Increasing Faith
Television Program**

or visit our WebSite:

www.faithdome.org